ISBN: 1886895-29-5
$9.95
Limited Edition
Copyright 2001
Poetry Harbor
Post Office Box 103
Duluth, Minnesota 55801-0103
www.poetryharbor.com

Artist Photograph by Sister Joyce Fournier
Cover Art by Pat Hagen

This chapbook was published by Poetry Harbor
with assistance from the Rose Warner Foundation.

Acknowledgements: *Peninsula: Essays and Memoirs from Michigan,*
The Christian Century, Your Life, Matrix, The Cancer Poetry Project,
The Re-Imagining Journal, The Dunes Review, The MacGuffin.

Special thanks to:
Marie Bahlke, Pat Hagen, Connie Wanek, Cathy Song, Pat Greenwood,
John Schifsky, Tamerin Horstman, and patrick mckinnon.

Poems I Never Wrote

Nancy Fitzgerald

"Writing is a process in which we discover what lives in us. The writing itself reveals to us what is alive in us. The deepest satisfaction of writing is precisely that it opens up new spaces within us of which we were not aware before we started to write. In the writing I come in touch with the spirit of God within me and experience how I am led to new places."

Henri Nouwen

For Elizabeth, Matt, Lin-ja and for their loved ones

Poems I Never Wrote

The Korea Poems

* from A Creature Who Belongs

Poems I Never Wrote

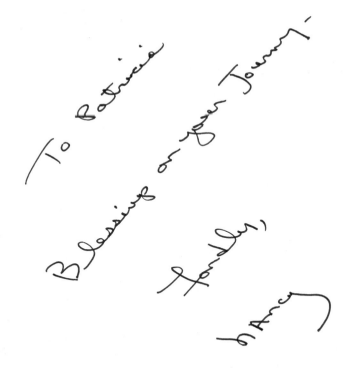

To Patricia

Blessing on your Journey!

Fondly,
Nancy

Pyramid Point

Shifting with the wind,
eroding old shapes into new
one grain at a time,
some dunes bury trees
and then move on,
sloping, rippling,
migrating toward
their angle of repose.

At Pyramid Point,
rain drenched the sand
and a massive landslide
moved what was on top
to the bottom.
Fluid and fickle,
dunes say, let go,
don't clutch,
let it slide,
make something new,
sculpt and dissolve.
Ridges into rivulets.

Bright Spots

The old man told of mermaids.
He said a farmer captured one,
hid her fins up in the attic,
kept house with her.
But when a great storm came,
and destroyed the cottage,
she found her other half,
swam out to sea,
returning only if it rained
to comb her children's hair.

The kelp lies on the beach
its tangled mass strewn
darkly on white sand.
The mermaid beckons me
to watery places, shows me
how to ride a wave,
to surface on a granite rock,
to spread out there and dry.

"Look back at all the bright spots,"
she says pointing to the shore.
"For you - yellow daffodils, gorse,
the shaft of light slanting
through the fog, white sheep
grazing on the hill. For me
the rain. There in the drizzle
amidst the fog and mist
I call my children to me."

She swims me back to shore
and dives away so singular.
I stroke the kelp and wonder.
Are her children glad to see her?
Do they answer when she calls?
Can they swim out to her?
How has she let them go?

Skijoring

Shaggy, sleepy in the winter sun
she wakes and wags when she sees
her harness. I pull it over her head,
pick up her forelegs, draw them
through the strap, tug it firmly,
snug it on her body. Now she frisks,
dances near the door, impatient
as I gather up the gear.
At the hill she holds up her paws.
I put on her booties then my skis,
then fasten us together with the line.
"Pull" I call "Pull," and she does.
I pole and stride and we glide
across the open field.

She's a different creature now
from the dozy domestic
stretched out on the rug.
Ice hangs in drippy globs
from her muzzle. Snow lays
on her back, her coat is bushy
from the cold, her nostrils wide and wet.
She is bred for strength and power,
not tapped by the toys we throw,
or barking at the garbage truck
or the comfort we take from her
resting at our side. Now
her deep chest and wide thighs work.
"No sniff - pull" I call. She glances
back at me, leaves sniffing and heaves
us forward. "Good dog," I say.
Each time I shout it I feel her tug.

When I fall, she looks intent.
Like a sheep dog who controls
with its eyes, she looks at me:
"Get up. You are leader of this pack."
I unscramble harness, lines, skis and poles
and we go again. She trots,
tail raised, we slide across snow.

The January sun is bright,
Lake Superior cold and blue.

When she spots two labs
across the valley
I grab the line and we soar
fast and faster
through frozen white
toward blue,
down and whooping
and I know I have gathered
all my joy into a single moment —
her ancient desire to pull
and my desire to fly.

Dove Bar

When Harold speaks, his words
once chosen and apt, now spill
out of his mouth like dice
tossed on the table, but no one
can add them all up. As he gestures
his fingers and hands emphasize
nothing - only the void of his mind.
He's gone to the fairies, can no longer
gather or harvest, decipher,
or ponder, reap or remember,
he's lost in a different stream of time.
We talk around him at supper,
he listens and then quietly speaks:
"I've been surrounded by good people
all my life." He states it softly
out of his depths, from a place
age never has touched.

I bring out Dove bars
and he smiles widely.
We bite into dark chocolate,
our tongues quiet with pleasure.
For the moment it takes
to eat ice cream together,
to suck the last bit
of sweet, to lick
from the stick,
for that instant we ride
the time stream as one.

Pauline's Hats

A coquette at eighty, perfumed and pert
she matched purse, glove and shoe
with dress, belt and bracelet.
Her face shown beneath rouged cheeks,
as she told stories of late husbands.
Men on her mind, she blushed
and jingled, dreamed of romance –
A Valentine creased at the edges.

At family dinners she wore gold,
broaches, beads, brimmed hats.
When she took off her boots,
she put on pointy pumps
over tinted stockings.

Now, in the nursing home
she sits slumped and drab,
brown baggy pants,
plain sturdy shoes,
her sweater hangs,
her scalp peeks pink from
a widened part, no perm
to hide her thinning hair.

From her wheelchair
parked next to the aviary,
she dozes in the sun and
watches captive birds
preen bright orange plumage.
Her chin rests on her chest
as they flit and primp.

In another place
her great granddaughters
try on "grandma's hats."
Floppy, brimmed, feathered,
velvet, furry, knit,
crocheted, one plumed,
they try them one by one,
sashay around the room,
and strut for all of us.

Nancy Drew

Nancy drew me in, modest young sleuth.
She slipped her hands out of ropes
in dark cellars, escaped from mean men.
She wore a forest green dress,
and flat-heeled shoes, she recognized
profiles, plunged into thickets, her dress
camouflage, girl detective, young sleuth.
She looked about, all directions were suspect.
She tiptoed, investigated, stayed on her guard
until crime was solved. She had chilling thoughts,
daring adventures, sixth sense, intuition.
Her hair snapped with electricity, she was
a beauty who turned romance away.

Nancy was steady, never bewildered.
Daring and smart she was more hardy
than boys, at the moss covered mansion,
in hidden staircases, by crumbling walls,
she recognized clues in old attics,
jewel boxes, graveyards and trunks.
She knew when to duck just in time,
when to run, when to wait there undaunted.
Her flashlight revealed all the traps.
If her batteries wavered or flickered,
she found a lantern, always had matches
in the pocket of her dress.

I sat on a stool reading her,
all lights turned on, kept turning,
so nothing could sneak up from behind.
And now when I'm all-alone
hear a noise in the basement,
I take my flashlight and go down.
I open the closet, look all around
and she's with me, my namesake,
bold brave and confident - -
Nancy who always drew me in.

Nun Study

"For fifteen years, elderly Catholic nuns have had the autobiographical essays written for their order in their 20s, plumbed for meaning in a scientific study for insights into Alzheimer's. As they have died, their brains have been removed and shipped in plastic tubs to a lab where they are analyzed and stored in jars. Research suggests nuns who have idea density and a positive emotional outlook may escape Alzheimer's in old age" *Duluth News Tribune*

At age 20 Sister Nicolette wrote:

"I turned like a daisy toward the sun
as my body swept along spirals of light,
like a swallow in scalloped time.
I saw swirling before me my childhood toys:
the doll house, sand sifter, yellow scooter,
all jacks and balls from the playground
my kitten that once wore a cap,
my Airedale who pulled a small sleigh,
tinker toys, teacups and saucers.
Mother's cedar closet beckoned me in
and the dresses and gowns I wore as a queen
joined sleeves and whirled me around.
Laughing and dancing I knew in my heart
I would never be as close to anything else
as these toys and my kitten and dog.
But now I am ready to put away childish
things, to take vows and love only God."

At 97 Sister Nicolette shows no signs of Alzheimer's.

To The Vandals

When I heard about the break in,
how you smashed a window,
took what you wanted,
used my bed and left,
I longed
to be there
sweep the floor
wash the sheets
burn sweet grass
in each room.

Peace, like a home,
is easy to mess up.
One rock, some booze,
greed. Did you not notice
how the trees inched
closer and floors
talked to walls and
rafters called my name?

Allusion

How much safer it is not to go to Mexico this winter
to practice Spanish with children lingering after school
in the warm village streets asking them "que tal?"
hoping they will answer slowly with short words.
How much better to stay home and sit close to the fire.

How much better for my friend to drive eighteen hours
alone in hopes of seeing her dying father one last time
after dreaming six nights of fiery falls from the sky
through trap doors that open under airplane seats
while the armed security guard looks the other way.

How cautious of my children to risk the blizzards
of Midwest November, take time off work to drive
home for Thanksgiving spinning on the ice rather
than sitting jittery at the airport wondering if the
terrorists have planned an episode just for today

as the turkey roasts and the pie cools and the table
is set, blessed for them. How prudent to pretend
we're safe on the ground, away from airports
protected by each other, surrounded by music,
stuffing, love, and mounds of mashed potatoes.

Isle Royale

Here days are measured by footsteps,
and how well the boot fits,
how snug the socks,
how flexible the arch,
agile the ankle,
quick the eye
to spot roots and rocks.

In the mist we set out,
lunch and water on our backs,
alone on the trail.
We lift the pointed head
of a Calypso orchid,
small as a fingertip,
expose its yellow beard.
It grows pink in the moss,
among the slick brown pellets
dropped by wandering moose.

A mammoth skull, cranial and white
eye sockets gaping, rots elegantly
in the weeds. I kneel and jiggle
a tooth to put in my pocket
to rub on ordinary days
to finger and reflect,
a rosary, an amulet, a charm.
But it will not come away
from the enormous jaw,
a pearly thing, secure here
from me and from you
in this secret wild place.

Goin' Down to Gary on an Ore Boat

We head out from Two Harbors with a load of taconite
around the Keweenaw, Whitefish Bay, The Soo,
under the bridge at Mackinaw, past the dunes,
and on to Gary Indiana. Chicago is a row
of giant tombstones floating in the smog.
We inch toward the harbor into the hopper
to unload. A recorded voice warns each time
the furnace blasts, smelting iron from ore.
We are told to stay on board, no one can visit here.
Warning, blast, explosion, spewing flames.
A worker scoops up coal in a bucket.
All day he dumps and turns, dumps and turns.
The pile he is shoveling down grows up from beneath,
the scoop an extension of his arms.
Trucks in procession carry limestone past the ship.
Through the night the pellets stream flowing
from the hold, the stench, the smoking stacks,
the warning voice, the blasts. Particles like snow
fall in the floodlights.

We wake up jittery, ready to depart.
The captain backs the thousand footer out,
turns it slowly North toward Lake Superior.
We head along the coast of Michigan,
Gary smoking at our stern.
The morning sun is bright,
waves follow waves.
The crew hoses down the hull,
the air is deep and pure.
In the dark, in the silence, in the peace,
the bridge is quiet. Wind washes over us
like so many unattended moments.
In the dark, in the silence, under the stars,
we slide by the Manitous on to Mackinaw.

Fissures

Some silences are deep as canyons.
Not to hear a voice or find mail
from a daughter, sister, friend
is an open sore, a daily gorge.
You stand on the edge of pain,
see her across the abyss,
but the ravine is rocky, vast,
too wide to yell across or bridge.

So you stay protected on the ledge
close to the edge, withdrawn,
alone, waiting in a stony chamber,
as the silence deepens.
And you wish for niches,
toe holds in the rock, ways
to climb down from yourself,
a way to bridge the chasm.

Navigate

The dead ones form a community in me.
I call on them to show me who I am.
They have helped in the past,
but they stutter now and keep silence.
No clues either in the sky at night
Nor in the wind or water.

When I'm least alert,
have turned to books
and living friends for help,
the dead ones rumble
like a diesel engine
churning up the sea,
set me on a new course,
and shine like a star
above the harbor.

Poems I Never Wrote

On the roadside one spring day
just off the pavement
a slender fox lay struck.
Its brother, sister, mate or friend
circled, sniffed and pawed
waiting for it to rise and leap
back into the woods.
Agitated I drove on to work.
How long did she wait there?

* * *

During harvest time on curves
between orchard and factory,
cherries slosh from vats
and spill out on the road.
Bright red for a day or two
abundantly they spoil.

* * *

The day I flung her ashes
on the water where we swam
particles of bone
settled at my feet.
Her ash floated on the waves
rising, falling on the crests.

* * *

At the zoo a chimp
caught my gaze.
For several minutes,
we looked at each other.
Then she summoned me
with her index digit
to join her in the cage.

* * *

In the maw of death
he lay skeletal, deep.
An old love song came on
my passion for him surged.
The painful damming back,
my drying up – his coma.

* * *

In David's garden flowers bloom
from hanging baskets, pots, the ground.
In June the poppies open like fire,
and iris stands erect as pines.
By July the eye can't count
zinnia, lily, rose, and pinks.
Something small and white,
a violet, grew hidden in the grass.
I almost missed it.

* * *

Outside the chapel
one cold night
I wait to see Sister,
any one will do.
She leads me to a quiet place.
"His chemo didn't work"
I cry and rage with her.
"Please help me now to pray -"
"We have been," she says.

* * *

When she was six months old,
I carried her across the threshold
of our new home. Outside
across the bay, a double rainbow arched.
Later in the labor room I asked for a boy.
The happy arc of pee.

* * *

In the bathtub, candles lit,
a harp and flute
a glass of wine,
the water hot and deep,
time and bones release.
Outside the wind and snow.
Upstairs in the loft
he watches basketball,
the space between us, steam.
When he hears the water drain
he comes down to me.

* * *

After the car flipped,
after the scan
I lay in shock.
He came quickly.
His jaw clenched,
his brow wet,
he absorbed me.

* * *

Pizza from the oven
a friend,
fresh oregano,
Greek olives,
puckered mushrooms,
blistered cheese,
a fire in the fireplace.
Outside the rain.

* * *

In church – a Tiffany window,
light glows through yellow daffodils
next to a blue brook. The hymns,
the gathered people, the prayers.
Amen.

The Source

Within four months
My friend died by suicide,
My three children married,
My car flipped and totaled,
My home was burglarized.

Finally there was silence:
The ritual of weekly walks,
Dancing at the weddings,
The clear water from our well
The stillness of my partner's eyes,

And from the grass, "Release.
Be rooted like the tree,
Receptive like the valley.
You never were the source."

Reflexology by Sand

Hard packed sand
at water's edge is best
one foot in, one foot out
diddle diddle dumpling
no more shoes
no more socks
no more boots.

Toes that griped
now grip pebbles
under the sun
step after step
they hum.

Ball, arch, heel
sand to toe,
toe to head
ball to lung
heel to nerves
zone therapy
energy flow

this little piggy for the sinus
this little piggy for the ear
this little piggy for pituitary
this little piggy the neck
this little piggy cries barefoot
barefoot, barefoot please
all the way home.

Immortality

I have ripened without him into this old age.
I am the one who stayed behind to raise
the children. In therapy I learned to say,
"I am going on without you,"
and now I've grown accustomed to
the early snow and the indigo's return,
and to his not being here.

But recently, sleeping near the ocean
when the moon was full, I felt the tide's
receding pull all night. My white
hair grew wild on the pillow as I spun
there waiting for the light to shape
the day, waiting for the light
so I could rise and walk the beach

in certainty. Here at home on summer nights
it's hard to tell the stars from fireflies,
and here the waters do not rally to the moon.

Old Cargo

Acknowledge your pain
in a safe contained place
like a ship where the mates
know their jobs and the watch
changes every four hours
all through the night
while you're sleeping,
and the captain appears
like a god at each port
on the rivers and locks
steering you all safely through,

There, aboard ship
where time is withdrawn,
between shores, consider your past.
You can lean on the rail
or sit at the stern and toss off remorse
to the gulls, drop guilt and grief
in the trail of foam where it churns
for a moment and then sinks.

There, acknowledge
whatever is broken
you must let it go.
Empty it out like the cargo,
unload it shovel by shovel,
then fill yourself up
with fresh water for ballast
before you begin the trip home.

In 1950 my father was sent to Korea by the American Government on an "electrical power mission." Our family was to have lived there several years, but the Korean War broke out and we were evacuated. Later my own family decided to adopt a Korean baby girl, and the experience of living in Korea came full circle. For her wedding on the shores of Lake Superior Lin-ja made, in the Japanese custom, a thousand origami cranes for people to take home after the ceremony. This section of poems is dedicated to her.

Korea:

Land of the Morning Calm

For Lin-ja

*"What use was it to have lived the past
if behind us it fell away so sheer?"*

Sisters in Korea: 1950

Her blond hair excited them.
They followed us on walks
when Ama pushed the carriage.
They clustered, pointed, circled,
chattering strange words, *"ch'ang baek han."*
Some were bold and tried to touch her.
Their hands darted out
to pat her head as if she were a dog,
which I had heard they ate from pots
not even knowing how to use a fork.
"They've never seen blond hair,"
Mother said, "they're friendly. It's Ok."
How did she know so much for sure?
We'd just arrived. They might snatch
her from her buggy, bind her to their back,
carry her away, offer her a breast in public,
feed her candy made of rice and
kim chee dug from buried jars,
dress her in a padded jacket,
put her feet in rubber shoes.
They might carry her *abuba* on their backs,
squat at the river as she slept, washing, pounding
their clothes with rocks, talking, always talking
in that odd way. They might make a goddess
of her baby beauty, set her on a mat,
touch her golden curls for fortune,
keep her as an idol, kidnap her for luck.
When Ama took us to the market,
hordes of children followed, begging, pointing,
reaching out to touch her hair.
Ama smiled proud and dawdled.
I walked behind and watched.

Playing in the Bomb Shelter

In Korea we played house
in Mary's bomb shelter.
A hump in the earth,
it was dark and damp beneath.
Her mother let us haul
down narrow steps
dolls, their clothes, cribs, stove,
tin dishes, table, and chairs.
Better than the forts at home,
a dwarf like child's space.
Flowers bloomed above us
wind bells rang
while we played snug
and hidden underground.

In America we had air raids.
When the siren blared
we covered neck and face,
dove beneath the desk
until the all clear buzzed.
But here underground
there were no raids.
We were safe.
Our mothers said so.
Until the strafes began,
the only enemies were boys
and they were Not Allowed.
We fed our dolls and changed them,
had birthday parties, played school,
planned over nights and swims
while up above the North Koreans smoldered,
gathered, readied an invasion.

Wanting the Blue Dish

They came with jiges on their backs,
triangle wooden frames balanced,
loaded with wares, instant bazaar.
If the cook said yes, they unpacked,
setting dishes, plates, crocks, brass
and scrolls out on a mat
all like magic off their backs.
They arranged stuff on our driveway,
then squatted there till Mother came.
She looked it over, sometimes pointed
at an item, went back inside
as if to get it or not was
all the same to her. Then Mr. O
began to barter, waved his hands
got excited. He took a lacquered tray,
turned it over, found flaws. The peddler
wrapped things up, then again unwrapped them,
and suddenly it was over. Mother got
what she pointed to. Mr. O looked happy
and the peddler loaded up, hoisted goods
back on his jige and headed down the hill.

Once I saw a dish so blue,
white lines across its curves,
I must have seen the lakes of home
and the sail's graceful curve.
Desire throbbing in my throat
I begged, pleaded, got out my coins.
"No" said Mr. O. "Too much. *Kapbissan.*
He will come again. Next time."

Weeks later he returned, unpacked,
and there it was amongst the brass and bells,
next to the silk lanterns,
the same dish still beautiful and blue.
Mr. O ignored it. He bought several knives,
a pot, spoke Korean, *"karangbi, ttugoun."*
Then as the peddler loaded up,
Mr. O picked up the dish,
as if it were a piece of junk
forgotten by the vendor.
Smiling he handed it to me.

I cupped the blue bowl
and for a moment
held the sky.

Blackout

"There is a skirmish at the border,"
my father said when he came armed
to take me home from playing dolls.
It was dark when we began to pack.
Mother used a flashlight
covered with her hand.
She said to bring
just what we could manage.
I packed a painted fan,
rubber shoes, a blue dish.
All night the flashlight darted
eerie and erratic, warplanes droned,
swooped and strafed, sirens startled.

In the morning our government
came up with a plan:
women and children
by freighter to Japan.
No men or pets allowed.
Full scale and without warning
the North Korean Army
invaded the Republic
with infantries and tank brigades.
They flexed killing muscles
while
like peddlers filing on the freighter
my brothers carried clothes,
mother carried the baby
we all carried food.

Evacuation

Refugees

On the bus to Pusan all the women wept.
Our mother sat, my sister on her lap
her face calm – I checked it often.
The wailing and wet eyes of the other women
made me wonder what she really knew.
They all held their husbands close when
they said good-bye, and then, women children
only got on a Danish freighter headed for Japan.

Despair

We set up camp on deck,
claimed a spot under the stairs.
Mother opened up the food
packed by Mr. O. "Peanut butter"
she had told him "and some tuna too."
Ever faithful, following her orders
Mr. O had mixed it all together
and spread it like mayonnaise the bread.
We gagged in disgust, threw sandwiches
to sharks, and Mother finally wept.

Typhoon

When the typhoon came,
we went to the hold.
Two nuns with spot lights
rotated them all night.
Mother opened K rations
she had stowed:
Vienna sausage, fruit cup,
diced up peaches pear pineapple
tasting all the same.
A cherry in the syrup
jelly in the sausage can,
the rolling of the ship
four seasick children,
the war planes overhead,
her husband held behind,
her belongings gone,
the dog a meal by now,
four days aboard the ship,
other's hungry children asking
her to share rice cakes,
fruit cup. As the typhoon blew
us across the Asian sea,
She held up.

He Belonged to War

In Japan we waited
for the war to end,
but it did not. All summer
things "escalated."
Father came to visit
and we hugged him.
But by then we knew
Mother was our protector,
Father belonged to war
like our dog, our friends Mr. O
and Ama, all the children,
who followed us on walks
our playhouse beneath the ground,
babies riding on their mothers' backs,
women squatting as they cooked,
the drum of laundry bats,
scrolls with tigers, misty mountains,
peddlers sharpening knives,
rice paper windows,
sliding walls and folding screens,
open markets full of brass,
honey carts that picked up sewage,
paddy paths, ox plows, coolie hats,
bamboo pipes and magic mats,
they all belonged to war now,
and we could not go back.

Arrival: 1973

"Why must your adopted daughter
be Korean?" the social worker asked.
Faces floated before me:
girls with bangs, bobbed hair,
close cropped to the crown,
walking to school in uniforms
white blouses, navy skirts.
I saw them in my dreams,
standing on swing seats,
pumping higher than the kids at home,
jumping rope, following the taffy man
who clacked his giant shears calling them
to buy rice candy cut from clear thin sheets.
I saw them every time an Asian child passed,
and I wanted one. "Because I lived there
as a child," I said. "I grew to love the people
and the Land of Morning Calm."

While we worked through immigration
waiting, waiting for bureaucrats
she stayed in foster care. For eight months
I was pregnant, alone in my own body,
measuring the way to Seoul,
measuring how she grew: now her teeth
are coming in, now she babbles, eats rice cakes,
walks, laughs, and bonds to others she will miss.
She was not smiling in her picture on our fridge,
scowling in her cotton padded vest,
waiting to come West to Northern light,
to find her place in a family constellation
she had no choice about.

A thousand silver cranes took flight
beside the plane which carried her.
When they placed her in my arms
I felt a stirring in my womb.
More treasured than a sack of rice,
awaited like spring rain.
A thousand silver cranes took flight,
and they have settled here.

A Moment the World Was Made For

They came to their wedding by canoes
along the shore of Lake Superior
as we sang praises to her beauty.
He sat tall in his dark suit
coming from the North,
she in white her veil streaming
gently from the South
they met where the water sparkles
and were paddled to the shore.

The harp rippled, the children gazed,
the dogs strutted in their bows,
some ancient words were spoken,
"for better or for worse" and
I give myself to you."
The people smiled and clapped.

They left hand in hand
and the lilacs on the altar,
in the baskets, on the bushes
sent their fragrance on the breeze,
and the sun, shining white,
warmed old love and new.

We are none of us afraid of deep water,
but float like tufts of cottonwood
on the surface of this moment.
He waiting in the North for her,
she coming from the South to him
their merging, our singing, the sun.

Flower Girl

The dress she wore as a flowergirl
was tiered in flounces of taffeta
that swished when she walked
and twirled when she turned,
it was yellow and fit only her.

She spun first to the right,
felt her braids take flight
the ribbons and bows,
then she twirled to the left
in her black Patten shoes.
She spun until dizzy,
yards of billowing yellow,
she turned and she twirled
then dizzily dropped,
knelt on the floor,
smoothed golden waves,
stroked shiny silk,
patted each ripple
until it was still.

Buttercup, goldenrod, daffodil, susan
marigold, tansy, honeysuckle, ladyslipper,
lily, poppy, sunflower, primrose,
she was lost in the glory of morning
she knew beauty and pleasure were one.

Profusion

In David's garden flowers bloom
from hanging baskets, pots, the earth.
In June poppies burn like fire
and iris stand erect as pines.

From hanging baskets, pots, the earth,
zinnia, lily, rose and pinks,
iris stand erect as pines.
By July the eye can't count.

Zinnia, lily, rose and pinks
a violet hidden in the grass
by July the eye can't notice
something simple, small and white.

A violet hidden in the grass,
I almost missed its elegance,
something simple small and white
amidst so much extravagance.

In June poppies burn like fire,
but by July the blossoms blend.
In David's garden flowers bloom
like Monet and Morisot.

Grower

All rooted things need nourishing
and there are some who know
how to plant new saplings,
how to prune a growing thing
how to trim its branches
so the heavy fruit cannot pull
it to the ground, how to release
the leader shoot so the tree
can catch the sun and flourish.

Though a grower must have vision,
like a parent with a child,
he holds sacred what the tree has always been
and is supple and straightforward in the shaping,
does the work and steps back,
knowing he is neither seed nor soil,
but the grower chosen for this task.

He stays at the center of the orchard,
welcomes rain, and gives thanks for fruit.

*Written for the inauguration of Larry Goodwin as President of The
College of St. Scholastica, September 1999.*

"Than Longen Folkes To Go On Pilgramages"

Someone in the loft touches organ keys
and the tourist gazing up at vaulted ceilings,
snapping photos of rose windows,
studying stained glass
quite suddenly sits down.

First the right hand lightly playing,
then two melodies entwine,
soaring up and over beams,
floating to the buttress,
settling on pews.
When feet stomp the pedals
bass notes drive relentless
toward a resolution,
slamming against stone
resounding in succession,
spilling down from apse to nave,
echoing from floor to ceiling,
filling up the cavernous space.

In a niche aflame
with candle prayers,
tourist turns to pilgrim.

In Praise of Travel

Sometimes a greater healing comes from leaving
than from staying at the tangled place called home.
Self finds it can, after all, lock the door and go abroad,
live as a stranger, released for a while
from its own reflection in the world.

It may walk through a terraced vineyard or
along a cloistered lime grove, past carillons
bursting out at noontime in a public square.
It may ride gondolas to the tops of peaks
hike the rims of mountaintops,
inch along a slippery staircase in a cave,
slip into shops of ancient textured things.

Once home again, the floorboards,
prison planks before the trip,
now lead in and out again.
And in the country self just left,
in a cottage never noticed
a woman tangled in her life
sits at her kitchen table
and longs to go abroad.

Every Mother's Son

"Her words still filled his mind
as they started their journey,
just as a mother's voice is heard
sometimes in a man's mind
long past childhood
calling his name
when one feels almost god enough
to be free of voices, her voice
calls out like a voice from childhood
reminding him he once tossed in dreams."
                    Gilgamesh (3000 B. C.)

She wants him for a friend in her old age,
one who knows her heart,
because she suckled him
and he felt her anguish as a boy
and knew her joy and was like
his father whom she loved.
She sheltered him and tried her best
to teach him how to use his gifts
for others and he had many gifts.
There were times when she
reached her breaking point
and raged at him and Anthony,
Saint of everything she'd lost,
and called upon her husband's spirit
to help her raise their son.
When he left home to start his journey,
she took off her armor, opened windows,
sowed wildflowers in the house,
gave thanks they had survived.

Ten years passed when in a dream
she saw him swimming in the sky
through the Milky Way toward her
and when a star fell in her field
it shattered into pieces and crushed
the Queen Anne's Lace, which grew
in clusters there. She tried to plant

the pieces, but her arms were weak
and so she asked her son
to share his strength
and help her gather up the star,
but he had no time
for her or her visions.

Her words still filled his mind
and reminded him of how
he called her as a child
when he cried and was afraid
and now he was a man.

There were no charts or maps
for burying a star, so she left
the pieces in the field
and in among the Queen Anne's Lace
Starflowers grew. Fragile and white
on delicate stalks they bloomed
under the moon and its three children
and in the evening she wondered
how she might have raised him
in a different way,
so her voice in him
was silent, so they could be friends,
before her heart went hollow,
before the stars and wild flowers
stopped their panoply.

Giving Gold

Since my hair turned silver,
I don't wear gold any more,
so I blessed the solid chain
passed down through my mother
and gave it to my daughter.
It gleamed on her
like honey in the sun and
linked her to another
woman who wore it with a
Cameo on a lacy bodice,
and one who looped it long
on a woolen sweater and
one who coiled it over silk
when she was feeling drab.
Now she must twist and
wrap circle, coil and loop
the amber chain around
her neck, arrange it
on her chest, and know
she is linked and linked
and worth her weight in gold.

Only A Fool

Only a fool would fail to notice
the indigo's blue as it flies
gathering light from the sky,
lustrous, shimmering,
it shines iridescent,
sings from its perch,
navigates North by the stars,
following the turn of the earth
on its axis, gleaming and singing,
perching and shining, only a fool
could fail to wonder each spring
at its return, carrying
the color of heaven,
knowing the way by the Dipper,
following the rotation of stars
steering and homing here
to this hilltop, only a fool
would fail to wonder if He
Kept his Promise to come back
from the Dead, to visit this place
as a bunting and watcher, flitting
and perching, singing and gleaming
only a fool would wonder.

**The voice addressing us is Grace O'Mally,
16ᵗʰ century Irish Pirate Queen, as she speaks
to Queen Elizabeth I**

Madame, as one royal personage to another
Queen of Connaught to Queen of England,
let me confess that I am sick to death of Bingham.
My domain has been the sea around Clew Bay.
I control a fleet of forty and the Western coastline.
My ships have sailed to Spain and Portugal,
Ulster, carrying goods from Connemara,
back with wine and spices, silks and glass.
It is true I have led attacks on merchant ships,
this is proper and as it ought to be.
They were in my waters.
I regret nothing, for I have served my clan.

This Bingham seeks to shackle me.
He has put my son in jail, impounded
all my fleet, insists on English shipping.
What an insult! I have navigated
through islands, reefs and channels,
drunk mead with chieftains and settled
their disputes and have for many years ruled
my own domain. I too long for the home rule.
But until then, Oh Queen, squelch Bingham
and give me back my land, my fleet,
my rights upon the sea.

I sense beneath your finery
an indecisive heart, a wavering.
I'll leave you with a story, Sister Queen.

My fourth child, third son was born
upon the sea as Turkish pirates plundered.
My captain came below to say
I must get out of bed, come on deck,
gather my men's courage as you did
the troops in Tilbury when you wrote,
"I myself will take up arms,
I will be your general."

I left my crying babe below,

went up and shot a musket,
at the wild Turks, and my crew rallied.
We over came the siege and sailed safely home.

As I nursed the boy I wondered,
had I called my men to help me
comfort and shelter the new babe
how would they respond?
Could they both fight and suckle?

Let us be quite frank, Elizabeth.
This Bingham is a gnat, a pip, a nuisance.
Woman to woman I say call him off.
Thus shall your subject according to her duty
remain in all obedient allegiance and pray
continually for your long life.
With this I take my leave:
put England's politics aside.
Let's make history based on gender,
an alliance no man can put asunder.

Communion

I am circling around God in orbits and glimpses.
You pass the cup of the new covenant
to me. In the quietude I take the food,
the bread and the wine, it is lovely and durable.
Our hands hold the tray, small silver cups,
we tremble that we might drop and disrupt
God's circling through the music and light.

I pass the cup to my neighbor, stranger or friend.
It is not at all like passing the salt or pepper
at home. It is darker and lighter than these.
It is a glimpse, though our eyes do not meet,
into the depth of the person beside me
as we look out from ourselves toward a God
who circles and orbits and spins us together.

Mountain Mantra

Mother mountain: your peaks
The trails along your rim
The flowers in your valley
The cows in your pasture
Peace I ask of thee.

Light and shadow on your slopes
Snow in your crevices
Ice flows over your mass
Clouds encircle your summit
Peace I ask of thee.

Guardian mother
I breathe you in,
Breathe out dark
Breathe in light
Soar and plunge.

My feet,
        one and then
           the other,
              move down
                your side,
                    step after step
                        I breathe you in.

Peace I ask of thee
Your strength, your silence
Your resilience in the storm,
I breathe you in.
May I walk nimbly along you,
The way of your peace
Is the way to mine.

Tell Me Why

You are at the center of the rainbow
and so am I no matter where we stand

Yellow and blue make green

The spider bites just one person
in the bed where two are sleeping

The finch comes to the feeder
and the indigo will not

A royal purple floret rests
on white Queen Anne's Lace

The fern unfurls and the poppies pop

Blossoms turn to cherries sweet and tart

The breeze blows in seconds into squall

Yellow and blue make green which
flashes some nights just at sunset

The Northern Lights pulsate
and birds quiver in formation

Every seventh wave is
big enough to ride

Apple blossoms are sweeter
than pear or apricot

Petunias stay so perky
and the zinnia droops

Tell me why
yellow and blue make green
and I will tell you Hush.
I don't really want to know.

Who Taught You Rapture?

Rembrandt's spot of light
Mozart's violin chasing the piano
the grain of oak awakening to oil
the indigo returning in the spring
the dance as a woman's skirt moves
across her thighs and her partner
catches all her ripples in his arms
the baby wet and warm from birth
resting after labor on your tummy
the rain
the wren
the work
the blossoming fruit
the day in bed alone
the day in bed together
the dog running down the beach
the poem opening like a rose
the taste of honey in Crete
your mother's lap
your father's laugh
the pancakes made for you
the silent night
the ease of death
the risen loaf
the perfect sail
the silent night
the stars
the breath
the moon
the silence
Who taught you rapture?

Read by Garrison Keillor on Writer's Almanac

The Meaning of Life

There is a moment just before
a dog vomits when its stomach
heaves dry, pumping what's deep
inside the belly to the mouth.
If you are fast you can grab
her by the collar and shove her
out the door, avoid the slimy bile,
hunks of half chewed food
from landing on the floor.
You must be quick, decisive,
controlled, and if you miss
the cue and the dog erupts
en route, you must forgive
her quickly and give yourself
to scrubbing up the mess.

Most of what I have learned
in life leads back to this.

Fresh Strawberry Pie

The berries must be local, Michigan are the best, but never flown in from California. They must be completely red through the center when you bite no white tips, firm, but not hard, the kind that wakes the taste buds back behind your ears. Bake a crust before you start, flute it if you want, and brown it lightly. Make the filling with sugar, water, cornstarch boiled for a while till it's clear. Toss the berries gently with a wooden spoon. Whip fresh cream and pile it high in a bright red bowl, pass it with a silver spoon. My friend said once she dreamed I fixed this just for her and urged her not to share it. It's likely pie, not poems, I'll be remembered by.

Line Dry

You hang out the wash
not knowing how long
it will take to dry
because so much depends
upon the clouds, the shifting
of the air, how it will lift
and flutter and when the sun
will reach each thread.
Diapers pinned one by one
along the line flap, snapped
by the wind, or sheets billow,
and all day you think
how your naked body
will slide between them
their scent fresh, crisp
from being aired all day.
And if by chance you're away
from home and suddenly
it rains, you know your shirts
and shorts underwear and socks
will all be drenched, but so what?
If you have to wring things
out by hand and bring them
in the house to dry, even
if it thunders through them
it will be all right.

Then there is the pattern to consider.
Maybe today you'll put orange by pink
and admire it when you glance out
or maybe all the socks will match up
side by side next to their partners.
Then there might be a tablecloth
next to the towels used by friends
who by now are miles away,
but you remember conversations
when you gather in their sheets.
And maybe one day you hang
all the dark things in the back,
the light things up in front
and you like how there is space

for all the wash because of how
you placed it and how frugally
you used the pins.

All day you notice a blue blouse
buttoned in the sun
and late in the afternoon
before the wishing star,
you take down the wash,
and bring it in the house.
Folding it you survey
the universe in a single glance
and give thanks:
for warmth and light, the breeze
and fragrance, for the ones
whose clothes these are –
and for silent tasks which bring
work and soul together.

About the Author

Nancy Madison Fitzgerald teaches creative writing and serves as advisor to *Out of Words,* the artistic/literary journal at The College of St. Scholastica in Duluth, Minnesota. She was nominated for a *Pushcart Award* in 2000. She has recently been a submissions editor of *The Cancer Poetry Project.* This is her third collection; the others are *An Inward Turning Out (1994),* and *A Creature Who Belongs (1998).* She lives with her husband Jerry and their dog Georgie on hilltops overlooking Lake Michigan in the summer and Lake Superior in the winter.